Contents

What Is Government?

A government is an organization of people that directs the actions of a nation, state, or community. A government has the **authority** and power to make, carry out, and **enforce** laws. It can also settle disagreements about those laws.

An important purpose of the United States government is to protect individual rights. In the United States, each person can believe what he or she wishes. People have the right to hold meetings and express opinions—even if these opinions disagree with actions of the government. People can choose their friends.

The capital of the United States of America is Washington, D.C. Most government activities take place there.

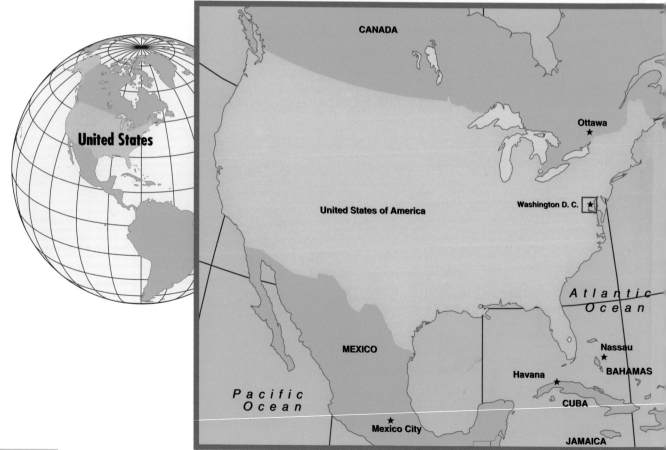

4

In the United States of America, people are free to ask the government to make or change laws.

The United States government has a responsibility to make sure that people are allowed to vote and to ask the government to change any laws they think are unfair.

The people who make up the national government of the United States of America work primarily in the nation's capital, the District of Columbia, also known as Washington, D.C.

In the United States, the national government's power comes from the U.S. Constitution. The Constitution is a **document** that describes—and places limits on—the powers of the national government. The Constitution gives the national government the power to raise a military force for defense, to collect **taxes,** and to make **economic** rules.

The United States government must make sure that people can choose the kind of work they want to do and can own property.

The Constitution

The Constitution states that the United States government was formed by the people, and that its power comes from the people who are governed instead of being ordered by somebody else. This kind of government is called a democracy.

In a democracy, people elect, or choose, their leaders. In the United States, citizens choose who will be our national president and vice president. They also choose who will represent them in Washington, D.C. Perhaps more importantly, citizens can remove from office a person in government who is not meeting his or her responsibilities.

The people who wrote the U.S. Constitution wanted to make sure that the national government did not have too much power. So the U.S. Constitution gives some powers to the national government and other powers to the states' governments. This is called a **federal** system of government.

Ancient Greeks and Romans each established a form of democracy for their governments. In ancient Rome, the Roman Senate exercised power by advising the government's leaders.

The Constitution of the United States is the world's oldest written constitution.

The first Roman Senate house, or curia, *was built in 670 B.C. In this painting, a Roman senator is shown addressing the Senate.*

The U.S. Constitution can be changed, or amended. An amendment must be ratified—agreed to—by two-thirds of the states. In more than 200 years, the Constitution has been amended 27 times.

Federal Powers	State Powers
Make **treaties** with other nations	Vote on constitutional amendments
Provide for national defense	Decide on voting requirements
Collect **taxes** on goods from other countries	Hold **elections**
Print **currency, mint** coins	Keep powers not given to the national government

Separation of Powers

The people who wrote the U.S. Constitution wanted to make sure that the leaders of the government did not have too much power. The writers spread the power among three separate branches of government that work together to govern the country. This is called **separation of powers.**

The executive branch is led by the president of the United States. This part of the government is responsible for making sure the laws are carried out, or executed.

The legislative branch is made up of the people in the Senate and the House of Representatives. Together, the Senate and the House of Representatives are called the United States Congress. The legislative branch makes the laws.

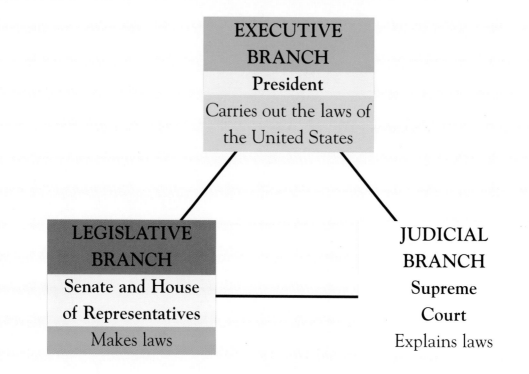

EXECUTIVE BRANCH
President
Carries out the laws of the United States

LEGISLATIVE BRANCH
Senate and House of Representatives
Makes laws

JUDICIAL BRANCH
Supreme Court
Explains laws

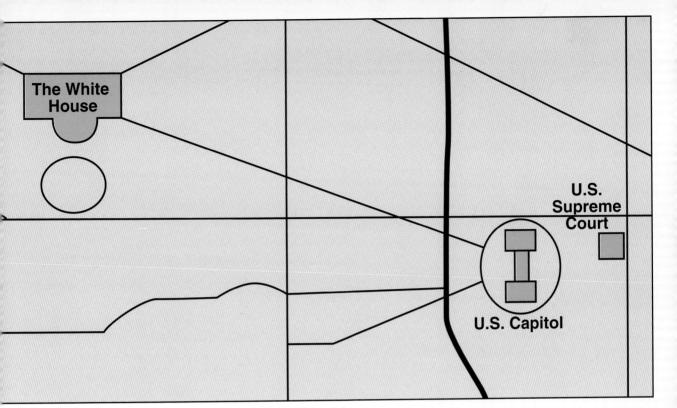

The White House

U.S.
Supreme
Court

U.S. Capitol

The Capitol, the Supreme Court, and the White House are near each other in Washington, D.C.

The third branch is the judicial branch, which is led by the Supreme Court. The judges—called justices—of the Supreme Court explain the laws and decide if any laws are not fair.

Each branch of the government has its own job to do, but the three branches have to work together. The people who wrote the Constitution were very careful to make sure that each branch of the government could check up on the others. A system called **checks and balances** keeps different parts of the government from having too much power.

The president, for example, can veto, or say no to, a law passed by Congress. The justices in the Supreme Court serve for life, but Congress makes the rules for the way things are done in the Supreme Court. Also, Congress can remove a justice from the Supreme Court if it decides he or she is not acting properly. On the other hand, the Supreme Court can stop a law passed by Congress if it decides that the law is against the Constitution.

The Executive Branch

The president of the United States is known around the world as the head of the United States government and **chief executive** of one of the world's most powerful nations. The president's actions are widely reported in newspapers and on radio and television.

The Constitution gives the president power and **authority** that no other person in government has. For example, the president is the commander-in-chief of the armed forces. This means that the president has the power to send the Army, Navy, Marines, or Air Force into battle. The president also has the power to make **treaties** with other countries. Some treaties are about ending a war. Others may be about the sale to other countries of products made in the United States.

President Clinton makes his 1995 State of the Union address—or speech—to Congress and other members of the government.

Medicines that people buy must be approved by the FDA.

The Constitution calls for the president to let Congress know how the nation is doing. Once a year, during the State of the Union address, the president talks about achievements the country has made or problems it faces. Sometimes the president makes suggestions for solving problems and asks Congress to think about them.

To be president of the United States a person must have been born in the United States, have lived in the country for at least 14 years, and be at least 35 years old.

The president may create special agencies to do jobs that are for the common good. These are offices that provide special kinds of help. People working for the Food and Drug Administration (FDA), for example, make sure the food we eat is free from disease. They also investigate new medicines to make sure they really work against an illness and will not cause harm.

The president may turn some jobs over to the vice president. According to the Constitution, if the president dies, the vice president takes over the position.

The President's Cabinet

The executive branch of government includes fourteen departments whose leaders advise the president. Together, these leaders are known as the president's Cabinet. The president has the power to choose a person to head a department. The choice must be approved by the Senate.

Even though the Cabinet is not mentioned in the Constitution, it plays an important part in the government. Each person in the Cabinet heads up a different department and has the title of secretary. For example, there is a secretary of the treasury, a secretary of the interior, and a secretary of agriculture. Only the Department of Justice (which includes the Federal Bureau of Investigation, or FBI) is headed by someone not called a secretary. He or she is called the attorney general.

The President's Cabinet

- secretary of state
- secretary of the treasury
- secretary of defense
- secretary of the interior
- secretary of agriculture
- secretary of commerce
- secretary of labor
- secretary of health and human services
- secretary of housing and urban development
- secretary of transportation
- secretary of education
- secretary of energy
- secretary of veterans affairs
- attorney general

President Clinton is shown meeting with his cabinet in the Cabinet Room of the White House in 1999.

The responsibilities of the Cabinet are varied. For example, the Department of State works mostly with other nations to make sure that the **political** and **economic** interests of the United States are protected. The Department of Commerce works to keep the business interests of the nation healthy and strong. The Department of the Interior is responsible for how lands belonging to the **federal** government are used, protected, and maintained. It also oversees matters having to do with Native Americans.

In addition to printing currency (paper money), the Treasury Department is responsible for investigating **smuggling** and the printing of **counterfeit** money. The U.S. Secret Service, which protects the president and vice president and their families, is also a part of the Treasury Department.

The Legislative Branch

In the United States, men and women are elected to Congress to represent the people. These men and women form the legislative branch of our government. They are responsible for passing laws that make the nation run smoothly and fairly.

Some laws passed by Congress protect the rights of individuals. Others are for the common good. For example, they set aside land for national parks and make sure we have clean air and water. They send help to areas that have been flooded or damaged by storms.

The United States Congress met for the first time on March 4, 1789.

Watch out for these two words—*capital* and *capitol*. The *capital* of a country is where the government meets. The capital of the United States is Washington, D.C. A *capitol* is the main building of a state or national government. Both the Senate and the House of Representatives meet in the Capitol in Washington, D.C.

Before Congress passed laws against child labor in the 1930s and 1940s, children as young as six worked from dawn to dusk, six days a week, in dangerous and dirty jobs.

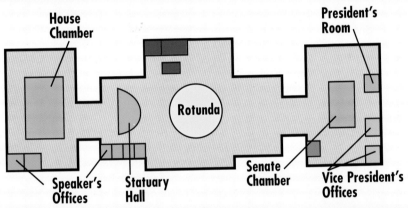

House Chamber

President's Room

Rotunda

Speaker's Offices

Statuary Hall

Senate Chamber

Vice President's Offices

The Capitol in Washington, D.C., was built in 1829. It replaced the original building, which was destroyed during the War of 1812. This view shows the inside of the dome of the capitol.

The Constitution gives Congress power and **authority** that no other branch of government has. For example, only Congress can declare war, borrow money, print **currency,** and establish **taxes** that every working adult in the nation must pay.

There are more than 500 people in Congress. They spend a lot of time talking and trading ideas with one another. Each person tries to do the best for the people in his or her home area as well as for all the people in the country. People in Congress also try to do what their **political party** wants. Because Congress spends time **deliberating** many of the items brought before it, it may seem to work very slowly.

The Congress

The U.S. Congress consists of two bodies, or groups, of people—the Senate and the House of Representatives. Both bodies meet in the United States Capitol in Washington, D.C.

The Senate is made up of one hundred senators, two from each of the fifty states. Each senator represents his or her entire state. The people in each state elect their senators, who serve for **terms** of six years.

The House of Representatives is made up of 435 members elected for a term of two years. Each representative comes from a different **congressional district** in United States. The number of districts a state has depends on the **population** of the state. For instance, people in Kansas elect 4 representatives to serve in the House, while the people in California elect 51 representatives.

To be a senator, a person must be at least 30 years old and have been a United States citizen for at least 9 years. To be a representative, a person must be at least 25 years old and have been a U.S. citizen for 7 years. Each senator or representative must live in the state that elects him or her.

Every ten years the government counts the number of people in the country. This count is used to help decide how many representatives each state will have.

California: 51 representatives

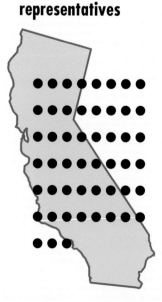

Kansas: 4 representatives

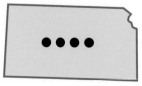

*During their **campaigns,** people who want to serve in Congress try to meet as many voters as possible.*

Senators and representatives can be elected for many terms. Some states tried to pass laws that limited the number of years a person may serve, but in 1995, the Supreme Court ruled that states cannot set term limits for Congress.

Congress meets throughout most of the year, from early January to late fall (early fall in **election** years). While Congress is in session, members live in Washington, D.C. But when Congress closes, senators and representatives usually return to their home states.

On January 4, 1999, the beginning of the 106th Congress, Senator Strom Thurmond of South Carolina was 96 years old and had served in Congress for 43 years and 1 month, breaking all records for service.

17

The Senate

The Constitution gives the Senate power and **authority** that no other part of the government has. In the system of **checks and balances,** the Senate must approve any **treaties** the president makes with other countries. It also has the power to approve the president's choices for Cabinet members, Supreme Court justices, and **ambassadors** to other countries.

The vice president of the United States acts as the president of the Senate. The vice president oversees any discussion or **debate** in the Senate. If there is a tie when the senators vote on an issue, the vice president can vote and break the tie.

The gavel on the left is the original gavel that was used to call the first Senate to order in 1789. The new gavel is on the right.

The president of the Senate begins a session by tapping a gavel on the desk. The gavel is a symbol of power. It is made of ivory and has no handle. The Senate gavel was a gift from India in 1954. It replaced the original gavel, which was old and cracked.

| Democrats' seats | Seat of the democratic leader | Center aisle | Vice President's rostrum | Seat of republican leader | Republicans' seats |

The place where the Senate meets is called the Senate chamber. It has one hundred desks facing the front of the room. Senators of the same **political party** sit on the same side of the center aisle.

The vice president sits at the center in the front, facing the senators. Below him sit secretaries and recorders who keep a record of what happens in the Senate. In addition, there are clerks and aides who help the senators keep track of the business of the day.

The Senate chooses one of its members to hold an office called sergeant at arms. This person helps keep order and reminds senators of the rules. The sergeant at arms also plans special ceremonies and **escorts** the president and visiting heads of state when they come to speak to Congress.

Above the chamber is a balcony, called a gallery. Here, visitors who come to visit the Capitol can watch the Senate at work.

The House of Representatives

The House of Representatives is sometimes called the House. The House of Representatives has power and **authority** that no other part of government has. Only the House can write laws that collect **taxes.** Also, if a high government official, such as a president or **federal** judge, does something that does not seem right, the House must decide whether to put that person on trial before the Senate.

The members of the House of Representatives choose one member to be the Speaker of the House. He or she oversees any **debate** in the House. Because there are so many representatives, much of the work of the House goes on in committees.

This is how the House of Representatives looked on opening day in 1997.

Mace   Speaker of the House sits here   Aisle   Clerk's lectern   Lectern   Leadership and committee tables

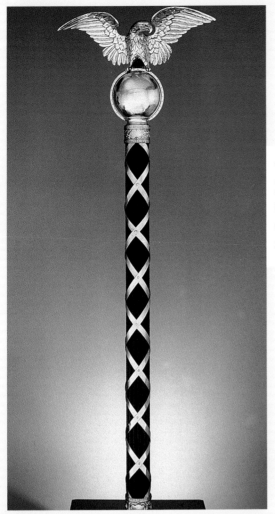

The Mace of the House is carried into the chamber each day by the sergeant at arms.

While the House is in session, the Mace sits on a marble table, called a pedestal, to the right of the Speaker of the House. But when the House is in committee, the Mace is moved to a lower pedestal.

The representatives, sometimes called congressmen and **congresswomen,** sit at desks in the large chamber. Desks and tables at the front are used by secretaries, recorders, clerks, aides, and the official called the **parliamentarian.** All these people keep track of what happens in the House.

The members of the House choose one person to be the sergeant at arms. He or she keeps order in the House during debate. The sergeant at arms is also in charge of the Mace, the symbol of power in the House of Representatives.

As in the Senate, a balcony surrounds most of the House chamber, from which visitors can watch the activity when Congress is in session.

Committees

There are many areas that need the attention of the legislators in Congress. In order to get all the work done, both the House and the Senate divide their work by forming small groups called committees. Each committee deals with just one part of Congress's job.

Both the Senate and the House have their own committees. There are a few committees in which senators and representatives work together. These are called joint committees. Many committees work on passing new laws. Some committees investigate events that interest the government. There are permanent, or standing, committees and committees formed for just a short time.

Standing committees in the Senate and the House
- Agriculture
- Appropriations
- Banking
- Foreign Relations
- Judiciary
- Small Business
- Veterans' Affairs

As doctors testify before a Senate subcommittee about juvenile diabetes, children who have diabetes wait to speak.

These witnesses are testifying at a meeting of the House Banking Committee.

Each committee lets the public know what they are working on and what kinds of laws they are thinking of making. People who have an interest in what a committee is doing can ask to speak to the committee. Sometimes a committee invites people to speak to them in a session called a hearing.

People can meet with the committee on agriculture to ask for help for farmers. Other people might urge a committee to pass laws against owning guns. Committee members talk among themselves and **deliberate** about what was said at the hearings. Finally they reach a decision about whether or not Congress as a whole should pass or change a law.

One of the most important committees in both the House and the Senate is the Appropriations committee. This committee sets aside, or appropriates, money for projects approved by other committees.

The Judicial Branch

The judicial branch of government is made up of judges, or justices, who serve on the U.S. Supreme Court and the judges in other **federal** district courts. The president appoints, or chooses, judges to serve in these courts, but the Senate must approve each appointment.

The Constitution gives responsibilities to the judicial branch that the other branches do not have. It is the responsibility of the judicial branch to make decisions concerning whether laws that Congress has passed agree with the Constitution.

The nine justices of the Supreme Court sit at this raised table, called a bench.

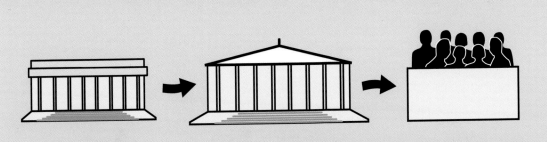

U.S. district court   **U.S. court of appeals**   **U.S. Supreme Court**

A case in the federal court system starts out at a district court. Each state has at least one federal district court, and one is located in Washington, D.C.

Federal courts also may hear cases in which the United States government or one of its officers is either **suing** someone or is being sued. The federal courts also may decide cases in which one or more states disagree with each other. For example, one state might sue a neighboring state, claiming the neighbor is polluting the air. The federal courts may also hear cases in which an ordinary person brings a case against a state.

People who are unhappy with a decision made by a district court can ask one of the twelve courts of appeals to hear the case. If they are still unhappy with the decision, they can ask the U.S. Supreme Court to hear the case.

The twelve regional courts of appeals are often referred to as circuit courts. Early in our nation's history, the judges of the courts of appeals visited each of the courts in a region in a certain order, or circuit, until they returned to where they had started. The judges, who traveled on horseback, were called circuit riders.

Laws passed by cities and states must not disagree with or contradict the laws set by the Constitution. The Supreme Court has the responsibility to determine whether or not a law is constitutional.

The Supreme Court

The Supreme Court of the United States is the nation's top court. It is made up of nine justices. They are appointed, or chosen, by the president and approved by the Senate. Once a justice is appointed, he or she serves for life. A justice may resign if he or she is ill or wishes to retire.

The president chooses one Supreme Court justice to be the leader, or chief justice. The chief justice is in charge of how the Supreme Court is run. The other eight men and women are called associate justices.

The Supreme Court meets from the first Monday of October through June.

William Rehnquist was chief justice of the Supreme Court in 1999. He is shown in the center of the front row.

The Supreme Court hears cases that involve constitutional issues important to nearly every citizen in the country.

During the year, the Supreme Court may be asked to listen more than 5,000 cases. Most of the time, the justices decide that a case is not important enough to take the time of the entire court.

Justice William O. Douglas served longer than any other Supreme Court justice. He served from 1939 until 1975—36 years. Sandra Day O'Connor, appointed in 1981, was the first woman to be named a Supreme Court justice.

However, the Supreme Court does listen to about 150 cases a year. All nine justices listen to each case brought to the Supreme Court while lawyers tell both sides of the issue. There are no witnesses and there is no **jury.** The justices **deliberate** with one another and reach what they think is the best decision. Often the justices write out their opinions in important cases, so that people will understand their reasoning. Not all nine justices need to agree in order to reach a decision.

Paying for Government

It costs a lot of money to run the **federal** government. The Constitution says that only Congress has the power to raise money for the United States.

The salaries of the president, people in Congress, and the judges in the Supreme Court are paid by the government. Millions of workers in the different departments help the government run from one day to the next, and they all must be paid. People in the military must be paid. Every space shuttle, every meat inspection, every mile of federal highway must be paid for.

Each year, Congress and the president work together to make a **budget** for the government for the next year. Sometimes it takes a long time for them to reach agreement because they have very different ideas on the most important things to pay for.

In 1999, for the first time in many years, the government produced a balanced budget— it did not plan to spend more money than it took in.

*The government prints **currency** and places it in **circulation**. It collects money from different sources to pay its expenses.*

Most of the money the government receives comes from **taxes.** In the United States, most tax is collected on what people earn for the work they do. This tax, called an income tax, is collected each year on the fifteenth of April. The federal government also collects taxes from businesses, too, but personal income tax brings in most government money.

In some cases, the government places a tax on specific products. For example, there are federal taxes on gasoline. For each gallon of gasoline a car uses, a few cents go to the federal government to build and keep up the highways.

No one, not even the president, can spend the country's money unless Congress first approves it.

Sometimes the government spends more money on programs and improvements than it takes in. This difference leads to the **national debt,** which has been steadily rising over the years.

29

How Laws Are Made

The idea for a law can come from a citizen or group or from a person already in Congress. The idea must pass several tests before it can become a **federal** law.

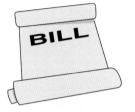

1. A representative or a senator writes up the idea. At this point the idea is called a bill.

2. A bill written by a representative is presented to the House. A bill introduced by a senator is presented to the Senate.

3. A committee reads the bill and finds out information about how the bill might work as a law. The committee reports to the House (or Senate) on the details of the bill.

4. The House (or Senate) votes on the bill.

5. If the bill passes the vote, it is sent to the other part of Congress.

6. The Senate (or House) studies the bill and then takes a vote.

7. If the bill changes as it goes through the other part of Congress, a committee of representatives and senators work out the final wording of the bill.

8. The House and Senate vote on the final bill.

9. If the bill passes the vote, it is sent to the president to sign.

10. The president signs the bill and it becomes a law. If the president vetoes, or refuses to sign, the bill, Congress can reconsider it. If they still want it passed, it becomes law.

Glossary

ambassador messenger or representative

amendment change to the Constitution, requiring two-thirds of the states to agree

authority the power to make people obey laws, to command obedience, or judge

budget plan describing the amount of money that will be spent and received during a given time

campaign organized effort to win election to public office

checks and balances system that makes sure different parts of government cannot become stronger than other parts

chief executive top person in the executive branch

circulation in use

congressional district areas of almost equal population that states are divided into for election purposes

counterfeit imitation that looks like the original

currency paper money and coins used in a country

debate to discuss arguments for and against something

deliberate to talk about in order to make a decision

document any written or printed paper

economic having to do with money and resources

enforce to make people obey

election process of making a choice by voting

escort to go with or accompany

federal the central government of the United States. also referring to a group of states that give up some power to a central government

jury citizens who hear evidence in a lawsuit and reach a decision

mint to manufacture coins

national debt money owed by the government

parliamentarian expert on the rules and conduct of a group of lawmakers

political having to do with government

political party group of people who have similar views about government

population total number of people living in a certain area

separation of powers system of government that distributes power among several branches and keeps each branch separate by making it illegal for officials in one branch to serve in another

smuggle to secretly bring into or take out of a country something that is illegal

sue to bring legal action against, to take to court

tax money required by the government for its support; may be based on property owned, money earned, or things bought

term length of time, set by law, served by an elected person

treaty formal agreement between nations

More Books to Read

Aria, Barbara. *The Supreme Court*. New York: Franklin Watts, 1994.

Bjornlund, Lydia D. *The U.S. Constitution: Blueprint for Democracy*. San Diego: Lucent Books, 1999.

Feinberg, Barbara S. *The National Government*. New York: Franklin Watts, 1993.

Quiri, Patricia R. *The Congress*. Danbury, Conn.: Children's Press, 1998.

Index